Extreme Machines

Powerboats

Scott P. Werther

Rigby

Powerboats
Copyright © 2001 by Rosen Book Works, Inc.

On Deck™ Reading Libraries
Published by Rigby
a division of Reed Elsevier Inc.
1000 Hart Road
Barrington, IL 60010-2627
www.rigby.com

Book Design: Michelle Innes
Text: Scott P. Werther
Photo Credits: Cover © Forest Johnson/Corbis; pp. 4–5 © Index Stock;
p. 7 © Tim Bieber/Image Bank; p. 9 © Bill Schild/Corbis;
p. 11 © Mike Powell/Allsport; pp. 12–13 © Yann Guichaoua/Allsport;
pp. 14–15 © Robert Holland/Image Bank; pp. 16–17 © The Purcell
Team/Corbis; p. 19 © Forest Johnson/Corbis; pp. 20–21 © Phil
Schermeister/Corbis

06 05 04 03 02 01
10 9 8 7 6 5 4 3 2 1

Printed in The United States of America

ISBN 0-7635-7877-0

Contents

Powerboats

This is a powerboat. It is one of the fastest boats on the water.

Fast as a Car

Powerboats can travel as fast as a car. They can go 60 miles an hour.

Powerboats are steered the same way as a car.

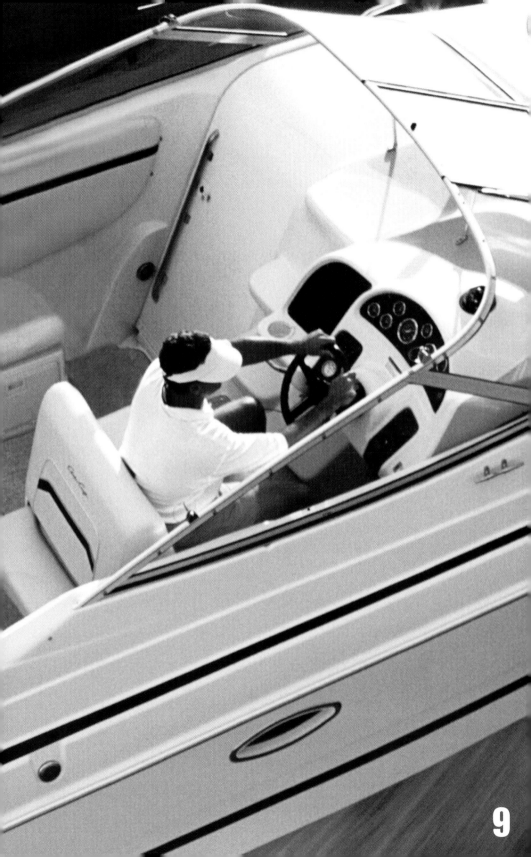

The Engine

Powerboats have big engines to go fast.

The engine of a powerboat
has a propeller.

Propeller

13

The engine turns the propeller.
The propeller spins in the water
and moves the powerboat
very fast.

Using Powerboats

Many people use powerboats. The United States Coast Guard uses powerboats to help save people in danger on the sea.

People also use powerboats for fun. Water-skiers are pulled by powerboats.

Powerboats can be enjoyed by people of all ages.

Glossary

Coast Guard (**kohst gard**) the branch of the armed forces that protects people and property along U.S. coasts

engine (**ehn**-juhn) a machine that changes fuel into motion and power

propeller (pruh-**pehl**-uhr) metal blades that spin in the water and move a boat forward

steer (**stihr**) to make something go in a particular direction

water-skier (**waw**-tuhr **skee**-uhr) someone who glides over the water on water skis while being pulled by a powerboat

Resources

Books

Boats
by Ian S. Graham
Raintree/Steck Vaughn (1999)

Eyewitness: Boat
by Eric Kentley
Dorling Kindersley Publishing (2000)

Web Site

http://www.marine.transport.sa.gov.au/
  kids/default.htm

Index